NUMBER KIT 2

All in pieces!

Fractions

British Library Cataloguing-in-Publication Data
A catalogue record for this book is available from the British Library.

ISBN 0-590-53591-9

Published by Scholastic Ltd
Villiers House
Clarendon Avenue
Leamington Spa
Warwickshire CV32 5PR

1 2 3 4 5 6 7 8 9   6 7 8 9 0 1 2 3 4 5

AUTHOR
Jenny Nash

SERIES CONSULTANT
Sheila Ebbutt
Director of BEAM (Be A Mathematician) which is supported by Islington Council

CURRICULUM LINKS
Ian Gardner, Maths Curriculum Adviser (England and Wales), Julie Parkin, with Edinburgh Centre for Mathematics Education (Scotland) and Michael Wallace (Northern Ireland)

The publishers wish to thank the following individuals and organisations for their invaluable help in developing the *Maths Focus* concept: Jayne de Courcy, Courcy Consultants; Dr Daphne Kerslake; West Sussex Maths Centre, West Sussex Institute; Oxfordshire Maths Centre; Edinburgh Centre for Mathematics Education; David Bell, Assistant Director of Education, Newcastle-upon-Tyne; Professor Geoffrey and Dr Julia Matthews

EDITORIAL TEAM
Irene Goodacre, Jo Saxelby-Jennings and Libby Weaver

SERIES DESIGNER
Joy White

DESIGNER
Anna Oliwa

COVER PHOTOGRAPH
© Grant Huntington for Scholastic Inc.

ILLUSTRATORS
James Alexander, Val Biro, Debbie Clark (Simon Girling Assoc.), Phil Dobson, Louise Gardner, Lorna Kent, Sue King (Simon Girling Assoc.), Derek Matthews, Janek Matysiak and Gary Swift

POSTERMAT
Anna Oliwa

Designed using Aldus Pagemaker
Processed by PAGES Bureau, Leamington Spa
Printed in Great Britain by Ebenezer Baylis & Son, Worcester and George Over, Rugby

CONTENTS

MATHS FOCUS

Maths Focus can be used to:

- assess children's knowledge and skills;
- offer reinforcement activities to develop understanding;
- provide enrichment activities to consolidate and extend the learning;
- develop skills and ability in using and applying mathematics.

DIFFERENTIATION

1 *Maths Focus* offers structured progression of content and skills through the Kits 1–5* and provides links with all UK national curricula. With a particular class or year group, you may use activities from more than one kit to cater for all ability levels. Each book focuses on a specific mathematical concept, with activities set in a range of contexts – including games, stories, problems, everyday situations and puzzles – so that children learn to use their mathematics flexibly and appropriately.

2 **Assessment activities** allow you to evaluate the children's ability to use and apply the mathematics they have learned.

3 Understanding is developed through two types of activity:
- **Reinforcement activities** – which increase children's confidence by concentrating on specific concept or skill and presenting the maths in a variety of contexts;
- **Enrichment activities** – which consolidate and extend children's learning in more open-ended contexts.

4 **Extension ideas** at the end of each activity offer ways for more able children to go further in their exploration of a concept.

**See inside back cover for overview of kits and curriculum coverage.*

offers ...

USING & APPLYING

Aspects of **Using and Applying** covered by each activity are given in the teacher's notes. To help with your planning, the grid on page 9 and the teachers' notes highlight how problem solving, communication and logical reasoning are built into each activity.

ASSESSMENT

Maths Focus offers two types of assessment to be used when you feel appropriate to plan the best way forward for each child.

- You may want to use the **Diagnostic assessment** activity at the start of teaching a concept to establish the existing level of understanding. Alternatively, use it after some initial teaching, to provide a check on progress.

- The **Assessment double-check** allows you to assess the child's understanding of the concept as a whole, to see how their learning has progressed.

FLEXIBLE RESOURCE

Maths Focus can be used in a variety of ways to support your teaching of mathematics and your style of teaching, allowing you to use the activities with individuals, groups or the whole class.

Use *Maths Focus* activities alongside a published scheme to:
- develop children's understanding of specific concepts in a greater range of contexts;
- assess children's understanding of a concept, and then to support or extend it with differentiated activities;
- focus on the using and applying aspect of the mathematics curriculum.

If you don't use a published scheme use *Maths Focus*:
- as a core resource when planning your own scheme of work;
- to teach and assess specific concepts.

USING TALK

All teachers' notes pages offer questions you can ask children to encourage them to talk about what they are doing. Use the questions while they are working to focus their mathematical thinking or at the end of the activity to assess their level of understanding. Most pages also offer:
- **Here's the maths** – explanations of the maths included in the activity;
- **What to look for** – diagnostic pointers to help you to assess whether the child has achieved the mathematical aim of the activity;
- **More help needed** – ways to help children are who struggling with the activity.

RANGE OF RESOURCES

Maths Focus kits come with a full-colour laminated postermat for each book. This flexible wipe-clean resource can be used with a number of the activities in its book and also as a general mathematics resource. Each book has a black and white photocopiable version of its postermat, to use with the activities and for permanent recording of the children's work. Extra postermats are available separately (see inside back cover).

The activities in each book are planned to use a range of mathematical resources, including counting apparatus, number lines and grids and calculators. Mental maths is emphasised throughout.

Fractions are not just a mathematical concept, but a part of everyday life. Children need to be familiar with them, and with decimal notation, which they will first encounter through their early experiences with money.

Here's the maths…

Fractions

What's involved

- In order to develop their mathematical competence, children need to understand the place of fractions and decimals in our number system.
- Children need first to be able to use the language of fractions in a confident manner.
- They need to learn that a fraction is part of a whole divided into equal parts and that the number of equal parts gives the fraction its name, so the name given to a fractional part of a shape divided into five is a 'fifth'.
- It is important to differentiate between 'a fifth' as a fraction and 'fifth' as the position of one member of a set.
- Children need to establish that two halves of an amount must be of equal magnitude, but that a half can be created in lots of different ways.
- Children generally encounter fractions first in a real-life context, so they will be familiar with half an apple or half a cake. They are likely to understand this as 'a part of' rather than 'one of two equal parts'.
- Even if children have understood the concept of 'half' they may still need to

UNDERSTANDING FRACTIONS

- Children need to understand that when a set or object is divided into equal parts:
  - the larger the number of parts, the smaller each part is;
  - the larger the denominator, the smaller the fraction;
  - some fractions are equivalent to each other, for example $\frac{2}{4}$ and $\frac{1}{2}$.
- These ideas are best developed through discussion whilst working on practical activities.
- There are many different ways of thinking about fractions. These include:
  - part of a 'whole' object;
  - a subset of a set of objects;
  - part of a quantity;
  - a point on a number line;
  - the result of a division operation, for example $\frac{1}{2}$ is $1 \div 2$;
  - an abstract number.

EQUIVALENCE OF FRACTIONS

- When working with fractions, children will realise, perhaps for the first time, that there are many ways of writing the same number.
- So, for example, $\frac{4}{6}$, $\frac{20}{30}$, $\frac{10}{15}$ and $\frac{12}{18}$ are all different ways of writing the fraction $\frac{2}{3}$, and so are said to be 'equivalent' to $\frac{2}{3}$.
- One way to teach this idea is by using geometric shapes in which the same fraction is shaded in different ways.
- Calculators can also be used to demonstrate that, for example, $1 \div 4$ gives the same answer as $2 \div 8$ or $10 \div 40$.

COIN RECOGNITION

- This is an important first stage in understanding money, and how it is used.
- Children need to learn that there are several ways of making up the same amount of money – practice in making amounts such as 5p, or 10p, helps children to appreciate combinations.
- Part of the basic competence of shopping is the ability to pay exact sums of money, or to offer an appropriate amount more than is needed, and expect the correct change.

WORKING WITH MONEY

- This provides useful opportunities to apply number and number operations in a familiar context.
- Money is introduced here as one of the first contexts in which children will meet decimal notation.
- Children need to understand that the use of money involves the concept of 'worth' – a more abstract idea than those of length or weight.
- They also need to recognise that coins are compared in terms of their buying power, not their size – some children also find it hard to understand that one coin can have a value greater than 1p.
- Early experience of money should be through observation and realistic rôle-play of buying and selling – real coins should be used whenever possible.

be reminded of it, particularly when the work becomes more abstract.

- They generally find it easier to understand fractions as parts of a continuous whole than as part of a set of discrete objects.
- A fraction of a continuous whole can be found by measuring or folding (in the case of 2D objects). Finding a fraction of a number of discrete objects, however, tends to be rather artificial, and depends on the fraction, and the number of objects being used – so, it is possible to find $\frac{1}{5}$ of 15, but not of 14 or 16.

INTRODUCING DECIMALS

- This can be done through the conventions of money and length in £ and m.
- Decimals will most often be encountered on calculators, and children will gain a great deal if they are familiar with common fractions. They can then gain an understanding of unfamiliar decimal fractions by comparing these with ones they know.

KEY FACTS

- **A fraction such as $\frac{1}{2}$ can be represented in infinitely many ways, all of which are said to be equivalent.**
- **A fraction is a part of a whole, not a unit in its own right.**
- **A fraction may be thought of in several different ways but is, essentially, an extension to the number system.**

KEY WORDS

fraction
decimal
equivalent
number line
division
whole
part
change

Curriculum links

This chart outlines the particular strands and statements from each of the UK curriculum documents for maths that apply to the content of this book.

The processes outlined opposite show how this maths is applied to a range of contexts and how outcomes are reported.

MATHEMATICS IN THE NATIONAL CURRICULUM (ENGLAND AND WALES)

This book covers the following statements from the Key Stage 1 and 2 Programmes of Study for Number:

Key Stage 1

◗ Pupils should be given opportunities to:
- develop flexible methods of working with number, orally and mentally;
- use a variety of practical resources and contexts;
- record in a variety of ways, including ways that relate to their mental work. (1a, c and e)

Pupils should be taught to:

◗ Develop an understanding of place value
- recognise and use in context simple fractions, including halves and quarters, decimal notation in recording money. (2c [part])

◗ Solve numerical problems
- understand the operations of addition, subtraction as taking away and comparison, and the relationship between them, recognise situations to which they apply and use them to solve problems with whole numbers, including situations involving money. (4a)

Key Stage 2

Pupils should be taught to:

◗ Develop an understanding of place value and extending the number system
- extend their understanding of the number system to negative numbers in context, and decimals with no more than two decimal places in the context of measurement and money. (2b)

MATHEMATICS 5–14 (SCOTTISH GUIDELINES)

This book covers the following strands of the Attainment Outcome Number, Money and Measurement:

◗ Range and type of numbers:
- **Work with:** halves (practical applications only) (Level A);
- **Work with:** quarters (practical applications only) (Level B);
- **Work with:** thirds, fifths, eighths, tenths and simple equivalences such as one half = two quarters (practical applications only) (Level C);
- **Work with:** negative numbers (eg temperature) (Level E).

◗ Money:
- **Use 1p, 2p, 5p, 10p, 20p coins** to buy things (Level A).

◗ Fractions, percentages and ratio:
- **Find halves and quarters** of quantities involving 1 or 2 digit numbers, for example by sharing (Level B).

NORTHERN IRELAND CURRICULUM FOR MATHEMATICS

This book covers these strands of Number from the Programme of Study for Mathematics at Key Stage 1:

◗ Understanding number and number notation

Pupils should have opportunities to:

(d) recognise and use simple everyday fractions and their notation in practical situations....

◗ Money

Pupils should have opportunities to:

(a) recognise and know how to use coins in simple contexts eg shop play; use and understand the conventional way of recording in money....

Using and applying

All of the activities in **Maths Focus** involve applying mathematics. This chart will help you to identify which strands of Using and Applying Mathematics are part of each activity. Problem-solving and Enquiry (Scottish 5–14 Guidelines) and Processes (NI Curriculum) are also addressed through these statements.

Activities	Problem Solving	Communication	Logical Reasoning
DIAGNOSTIC ASSESSMENT			
Colouring fractions (FRACTIONS)	Finding appropriate fractions	Talking about the fractions used	Explaining how to use fractions
Shopping (MONEY)	Selecting the appropriate coins required for the task	Recording findings and discussing results	Predicting what money will be left before making the purchase
ASSESSMENT DOUBLE-CHECK			
Fractions of things (FRACTIONS)	Using knowledge of fractions to fold paper into halves and quarters Completing the task	Using the convention for recording fractions Explaining results	
How much money? (MONEY)	Selecting appropriate strategies for calculation, such as counting on	Using appropriate language relating to money exchange Recording using pictures or numbers	Predicting the amount of change before using the coins Working out a way of checking results
REINFORCEMENT ACTIVITIES			
All in the bag		Using the language of simple fractions	Responding to 'What if...' questions
Halve it... quarter it	Deciding how to organise an investigation		
Uncover the board		Reporting orally on the results of playing the fractions game	
How to find half	Deciding how to use mathematical equipment to solve a problem		
Would you rather have...?	Deciding how to use equipment to solve a problem	Using the language of simple fractions	Responding to 'What if...' questions
Make 10p	Deciding how to use coins in the context of a game		Developing strategies for playing games
Shake the cup	Deciding how to find the smallest number of coins for a given amount	Recording coin values	
ENRICHMENT ACTIVITIES			
Hidden fractions	Deciding how to begin a problem		Making decisions about fractions
Fraction number lines		Reading, writing and using the language of simple fractions in context	
Coins in the circle	Finishing a set task	Discussing simple money problems	
How much more?	Deciding how to use money to solve problems	Inventing simple ways of recording	
Build up game	Following rules and working independently within a group	Responding appropriately to questions	Predicting who will win a game
Calculator decimals	Using the calculator correctly and following appropriate lines of enquiry	Discussing work with others	Spotting number patterns and making generalisations Using mental methods to predict solutions
Circle challenge	Picking an appropriate piece and appreciating the strategies involved	Asking and answering questions using the appropriate vocabulary	Counting on to calculate how much is required to finish

Colouring fractions

Key aims

- To discover how confident a child is about:
  - understanding that fractions are equal parts of a whole;
  - finding fractions of objects;
  - finding fractions of sets.

What you need

- 1 activity sheet for each child
- pencils for writing and colouring

The activity

- Discuss fractions with the children.
- Give each child a copy of the activity sheet to complete.
- Let them work independently as far as possible, helping with reading as necessary.

Assessing understanding

- Look for the following to indicate that the children are ready for **Enrichment activities**. They may:
  - be able to identify and find fractions of objects and sets confidently;
  - be able to explain the reasons for their decisions;
  - demonstrate that they understand equivalence;
  - show they understand that fractional parts are equal.
- Look for the following to indicate that the children are in need of further work on the concept of fractions. They may:
  - lack confidence and look for reassurance;
  - be unable to explain or discuss the reasons for their decisions and choices;
  - think that a shape cut in two has been halved regardless of the size of the pieces;
  - be unable to identify or find fractions of objects or sets.

Children who need more help

- Children who are unable to find fractions of shapes need further work to establish a basic understanding of fractions. Go on to **Reinforcement activities** 'All in the bag' (page 18) and 'Would you rather have?' (page 26). Children who fail to understand that two quarters are equal to one half need practical experience, as provided in 'All in the bag' (page 18) and 'Uncover the board' (page 22). Children who have difficulty finding fractions of sets may be helped by the activity 'Halve it .. quarter it' (page 20).

ASSESSING USING & APPLYING

PROBLEM SOLVING

- Can the child find appropriate fractions?

COMMUNICATION

- Can the children talk about the fractions they have used?

LOGICAL REASONING

- Can the children explain how they used fractions?

TALK ABOUT

- *'Can anyone remember what a fraction is?'*
- *'Why did you colour in that part of the shape?'*
- *'How many quarters will there be?'*
- *'What name do we give to each part if a shape has been cut into three equal parts?'*

HERE'S THE MATHS

- The ability to find a given fraction of a shape, or a number of objects, is an important and useful aspect of the idea of fractions.
- Children need plenty of practical experience to help them see fractions, in the abstract sense, as numbers that can be placed on a number line.
- The idea of equivalence introduces the notion that there are infinitely many ways of representing the same number.

Name ______________________

Colouring fractions

Colour one half of each of these shapes.

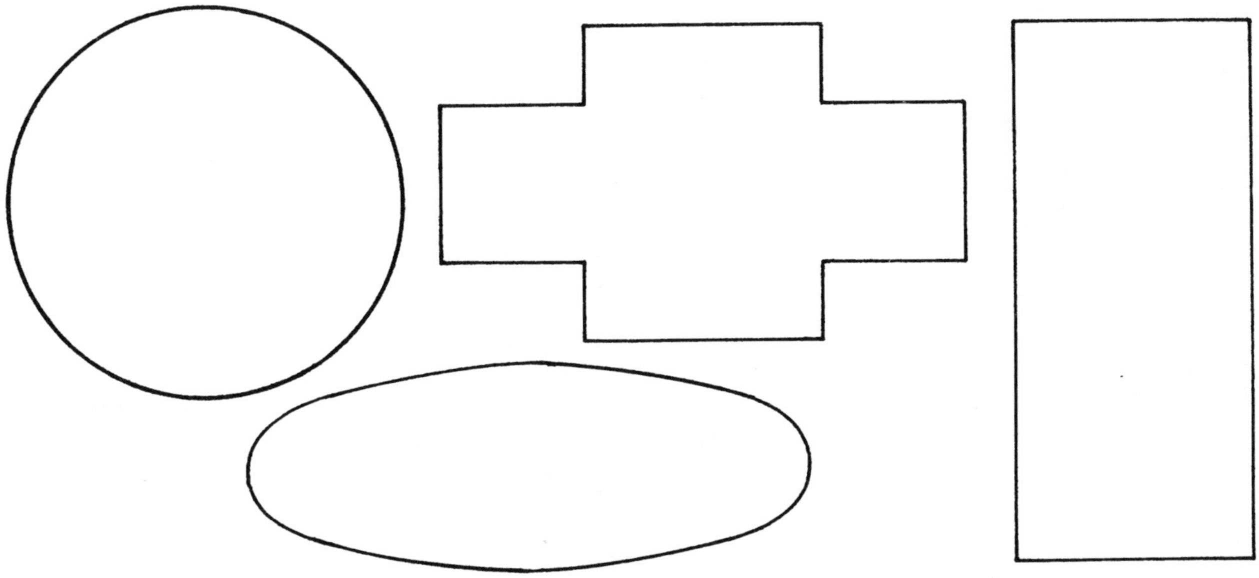

Colour one half of each of these shapes.
Colour different parts for each one.

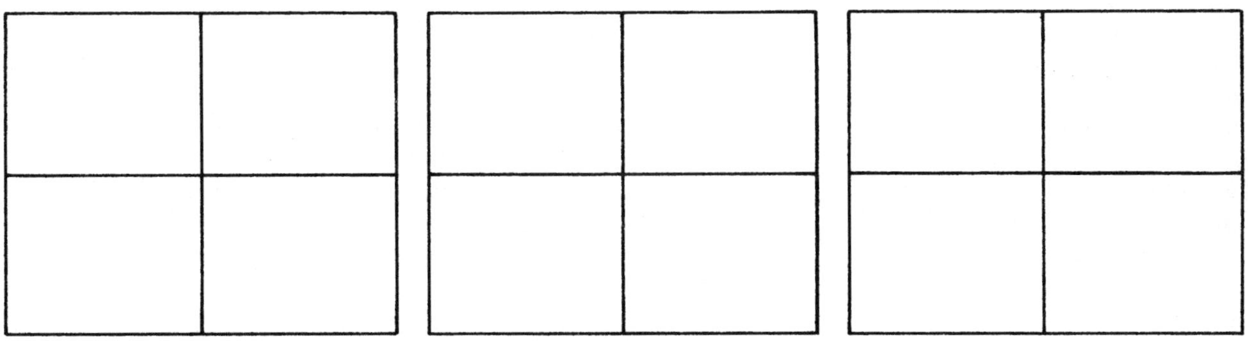

Colour one quarter of each of these shapes.

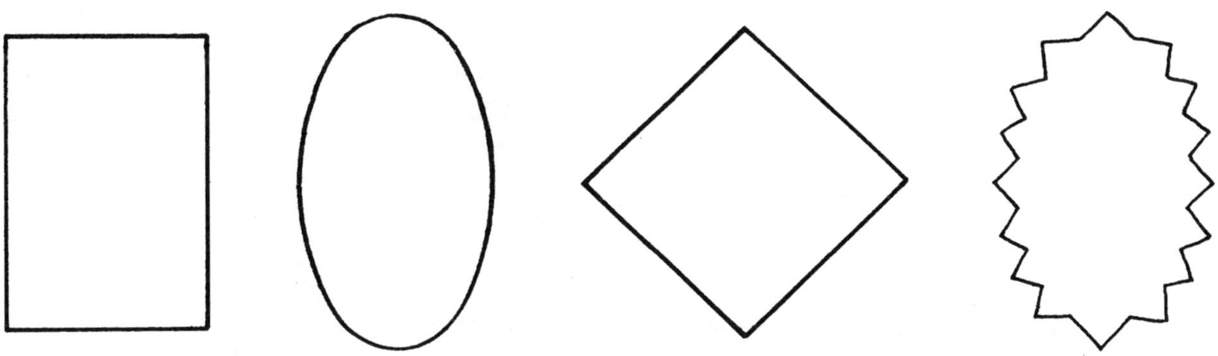

Shopping

Key aims

- To consider how confident a child is about:
  - using coins of different denominations;
  - providing appropriate amounts of money;
  - counting how much money is left.

What you need

- 1 activity sheet per child
- sets of coins – 10p, 5p, 2p, 2p, 1p – one for each child
- a selection of items, priced with amounts less than 20p

Organisation

- This activity can be conducted with groups if you have access to a range of items of various prices. Alternatively, fill the first column with drawings of priced items.

The activity

- Give each child an activity sheet and a set of coins.
- Tell them that the total amount they each have is 20p, and that they will be using these coins to make the exact amounts of money needed to buy the items displayed.
- Explain how they can record the coins they use to 'buy' each item in the middle column. They must also record how much money they have left after they have 'bought' the item.
- Work through one example, without teaching the skills. Ask the children to group their money, then to fill in the activity sheet. Observe how the children handle the coins to calculate the totals they have and how much money is remaining.

Assessing understanding

- Look for the following to tell you that the children are ready for **Enrichment activities**. They may appreciate that the coins carry different values; present amounts accurately; complete both columns of the sheet; observe that the money used and the money left always total 20p.
- Look for the following to indicate that the children are in need of further work on the concept of money. They may be unable to discriminate between the coins and unclear of the number sequence between 10 and 20.

Children who need more help

- Try **Reinforcement activity** 'Make 10p' (page 28) which encourages children to explore combinations of coins within that amount and develops confidence with 1p, 2p and 5p coins.

USING & APPLYING / ASSESSING

PROBLEM SOLVING
- Can the child select the appropriate coins required for the task?

COMMUNICATION
- Can the child record findings on the sheet and discuss the results with you?

LOGICAL REASONING
- Can the child predict what money will be left before making the purchase?

TALK ABOUT

- *'How did you know which coins to use?'*
- *'Have you checked your answers?'*
- *'Do you know how you could work out how much money you would have left without putting out the coins?'*

HERE'S THE MATHS

- Using money in everyday transactions is an essential part of living in a modern world.
- It depends on being able to select appropriate coins or notes for any specific purchase, without handing over redundant coins.
- It is also important to recognise that the correct amount of change has been given.
- It is through money that children will first experience decimal notation.

Name ______________________________

Shopping

Item	Coins used	Coins left

Fractions of things

Key aims

- To assess the extent to which children can:
- find fractions of sets;
- understand that fractions are equal parts of a whole.

What you need

- 1 activity sheet for each child
- counters in a box or bag
- pencils
- dice numbered 2, 4, 6, 8, 12, 16

Organisation

- This assessment is a game with two different versions called 'Halves' and 'Quarters' and is played in groups of two, three or four.

The activity

- Begin the activity by taking a sheet of paper and folding it to show first a half, then a quarter.
- Discuss the activity sheet with the children.
- Observe them while they play the game.
- Once they have played the game halving the set, repeat the activity, with the children quartering the set and keeping a quarter of the counters where this is possible, otherwise all the counters must be put back.
- Children could go on to find thirds, or any other fraction on which they have been working.

Assessing understanding

- Look for an ability to:
- find fractions of sets and shapes confidently;
- explain how they have found fractional parts;
- find halves and quarters.

USING & APPLYING ASSESSING

PROBLEM SOLVING

- Can the child:
- use knowledge of fractions to fold paper into halves and quarters?
- complete the task?

COMMUNICATION

- Can the child:
- use the convention for recording fractions?
- explain results?

TALK ABOUT

- *'How do you know that the part you have labelled is a quarter?'*
- *'Can you think of another way to fold the paper to show a half?'*
- *'Is there a way to check whether you have found a quarter of the set?'*

HERE'S THE MATHS

- Halves and quarters are the most commonly-used fractions and familiarity with them will lay a good foundation for understanding other fractions.
- The notion that a quarter can be found by taking one half of a half is important.

Name ______________________

Fractions of things

Play 'Halves'.
Take a dice numbered 2, 4, 6, 8, 12, 16.
Collect some counters and put them in a box or bag.

Take turns to throw the dice and collect that number of counters.

Find half of the set of counters you have collected and put them back in the bag.
The first person to collect exactly 25 counters wins.
Now try playing 'Quarters'.

ASSESSING USING & APPLYING

PROBLEM SOLVING

◗ Does the child select appropriate strategies for calculation, such as counting on?

COMMUNICATION

◗ Does the child:

- use appropriate language relating to money exchange?
- record using pictures or numbers?

LOGICAL REASONING

◗ Can the child:

- predict the amount of change before using the coins?
- work out a way of checking results?

TALK ABOUT

- *'How do you find the right coins'*
- *'How do you work out the change?'*
- *'How might you check your answers?'*

How much money?

Key aims

◗ To discover how confident a child is about:

- selecting coins for totals up to £1;
- strategies for calculating change from £1.

What you need

◗ 1 copy of the activity sheet for each child

◗ a set of coins made up of 50p, 2 × 20p, 2 × 10p, 2 × 5p, 2 × 2p, 2 × 1p, for each child

◗ a selection of items with price tags (all under £1)

Organisation

◗ The selected set of coins can be used to give any amount up to £1. Using a minimal set encourages children to use all of the denominations and provides a manageable quantity of coins to work with.

◗ Focus on children individually to see how well they apply the sub-skills involved in handling money. Ask them questions to confirm your observations.

The activity

◗ Give out the activity sheets and lay out the priced items.

◗ Tell the children that they will need to work out how much change would be given for each item if a customer paid £1. They will each have a set of coins which range from 1p to 50p and provide more money than they actually need.

◗ Take the children through one example, demonstrating the 'counting on' approach for calculating change. Then leave the children to work through the task alone.

◗ Some children may calculate change using an individual approach. This can lead to interesting discussion.

Assessing understanding

◗ Look for:

- confidence in counting on to the nearest 5p, 10p and so on.
- mental agility with numbers to 100.

Children who need more help

◗ Children who have difficulty with this task may need some consolidatory work on counting on within 20p. Return to the **Diagnostic activity** 'Shopping' on page 12, but this time provide more coins than required so that children are forced to use some method of calculation.

Name ______________________________

How much money?

Amount	Coins used	Change from £1

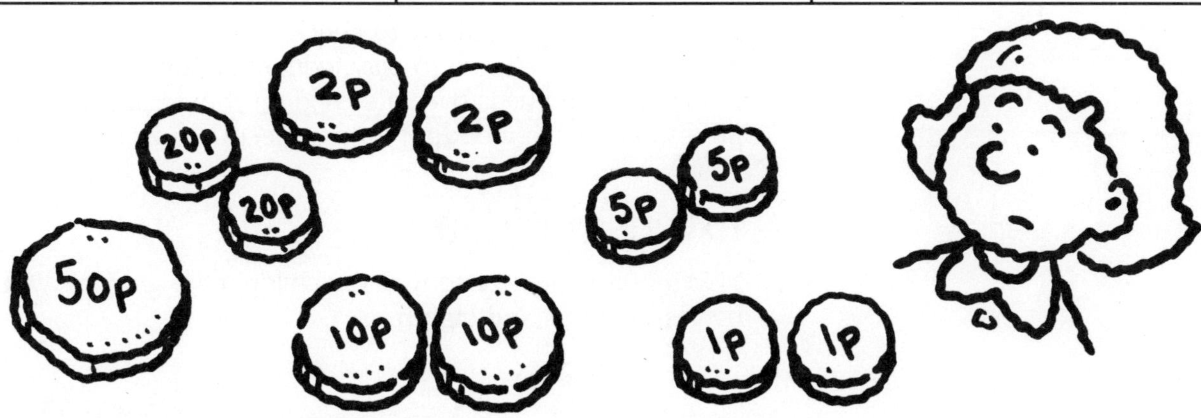

All in the bag

USING & APPLYING

COMMUNICATION
- Use the language of simple fractions.

LOGICAL REASONING
- Respond to 'What if...' questions.

TALK ABOUT

- *'What would happen if you had pulled out a half instead of a quarter?'*
- *'What fraction do you need to finish?*
- *'Would any other fractions work?'*
- *'How much have you got so far?'*

HERE'S THE MATHS

- This activity deals with fractions as part of a whole, and with the idea that, for example, two quarters are equivalent to one half.

WHAT TO LOOK FOR

- Do the children see that two quarters are the same as one half?
- Can they tell you how much they have so far?

MORE HELP NEEDED

- Give the children a 'bingo' board of whole shapes on to which they fit the shapes they pull out of the bag.

Key aims

- To identify fractions of objects by combining fractions of shapes to make new shapes.
- To order mixed number fractions.
- To introduce the idea of equivalence.
- To use the language of fractions.

What you need

- 1 activity sheet and 1 copy of page 46 for each pair of children
- 1 postermat or the photocopiable version on page 48 between two children
- scissors – 1 pair between two children
- an opaque bag for each pair
- pencils and paper

Organisation

- Ensure that there are enough scissors for each pair to be able to cut out their cards from the photocopiable sheet.
- Cut rectangles, circles and triangles of different sizes from scrap paper.
- Group the children around you.

The activity

- Remind the children about halves and quarters by folding and cutting scrap paper.
- Give the children the scrap paper pieces to halve and quarter and encourage them to use the correct language. If the children do not mention it, point out that two quarters of a shape are the same size as one half of the same shape.
- Show the children that the rectangular half and quarter cards fit the squares on the postermat.
- Talk the children through the instructions for the game on the activity sheet, then ask them to cut out the fraction pieces.
- Watch each pair initially to check they understand the game, then leave them to play independently.
- When the game is over the children should put their sets of pieces in order to work out whose pieces are worth the most.

Extension idea

- Extend the activity so that the children are working with halves, quarters and eighths.

Name ______________________

All in the bag

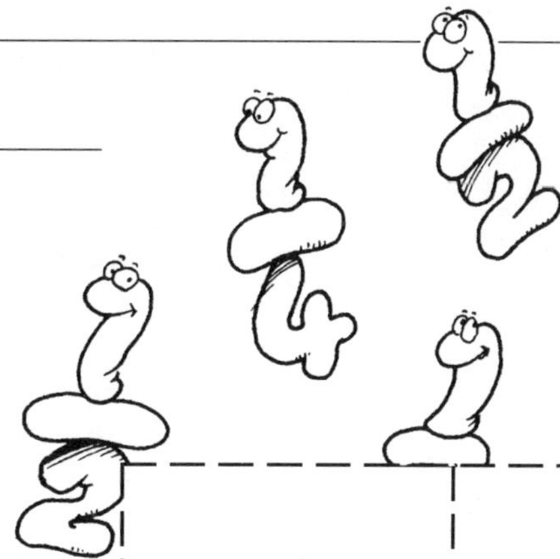

A game for two players.

Cut out the half and quarter fraction pieces on each of your sheets and put them all in the bag.

Take turns to pull out three fraction pieces from the bag.

Each time, put them together on your postermat outlines to make as many whole ones as possible.

Keep the pieces used to make each whole one together. Do not use them again.

Take three turns each.

Then count up how many whole ones and how many pieces you have altogether.

$\frac{1}{2}$	$\frac{1}{2}$

$\frac{1}{2}$	$\frac{1}{2}$

$\frac{1}{2}$	$\frac{1}{2}$

$\frac{1}{2}$	$\frac{1}{2}$

Halve it... quarter it

Key aim

- To find halves and quarters of shapes and sets of items.

What you need

- 1 activity sheet for each child
- colouring pencils
- various shapes cut from scrap paper
- some cubes or counters

Organisation

- Once the initial group work has been done children can work in pairs or individually as appropriate.
- If the children are to work in pairs they could either work on one activity sheet between them, or complete a sheet each, discussing how to colour it as they go along.

The activity

- Talk to the children about fractions and discuss ways to halve the paper shapes.
- Work with the group to find half of a set of six counters or cubes. They may suggest halving an array or dividing the set by two. Discuss both methods and point out that the answer is the same whichever way is chosen.
- Move on to halve amounts other than six – help the children to use both methods of halving and encourage them to say the appropriate number sentence, for example 'half of 8 is 4'.
- When the children are confident about finding half of a range of numbers, ask them to find quarters.
- Hand out copies of the activity sheet and ask the children to show different ways to colour half of each shape or a quarter of each set. If they want to colour parts of each shape in a set encourage this.

Extension idea

- Use the photocopiable version of the postermat (page 48). Ask the children to colour halves, then quarters of all the shapes in as many different ways as possible.

USING & APPLYING

PROBLEM SOLVING
- Decide how to organise an investigation.

TALK ABOUT

- *'How will you colour half of this shape?'*
- *'What fraction of the set are you colouring?'*
- *'How many more will you colour?'*

HERE'S THE MATHS

- This activity deals with finding simple fractions of both shapes and sets of objects.

WHAT TO LOOK FOR

- Can the children colour half of each shape?
- Can the children use their own strategies for finding half of a number of objects?
- Can they also find a quarter?
- Can they do the same with drawings of objects?

MORE HELP NEEDED

- Allow the children to use objects to help them complete the activity sheets.

Name ____________________

Halve it... quarter it

Colour half of each shape.

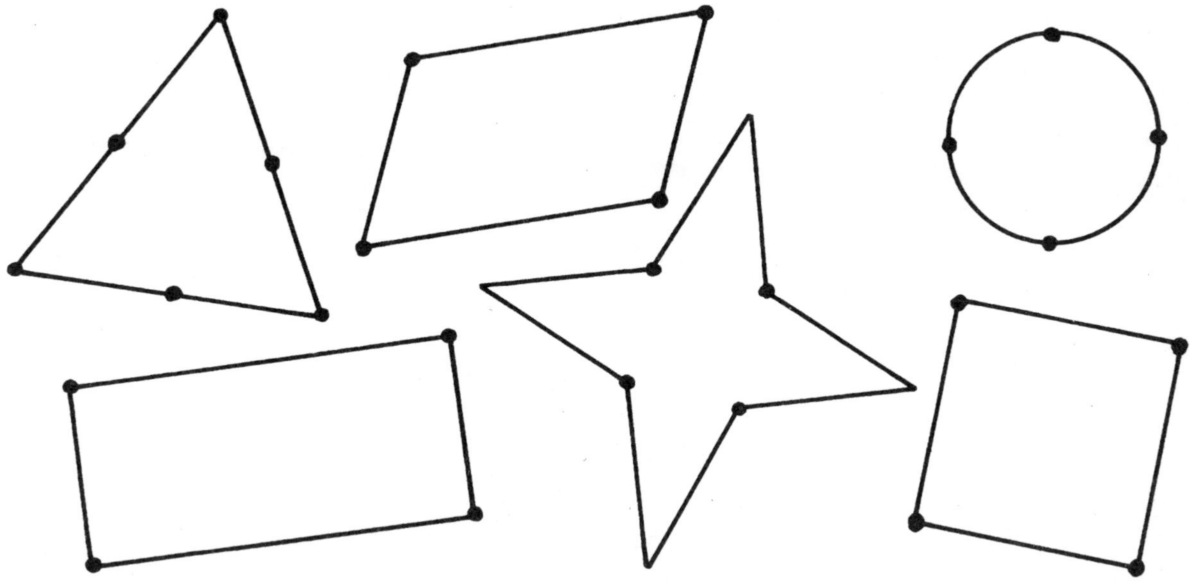

Colour a quarter of each set.

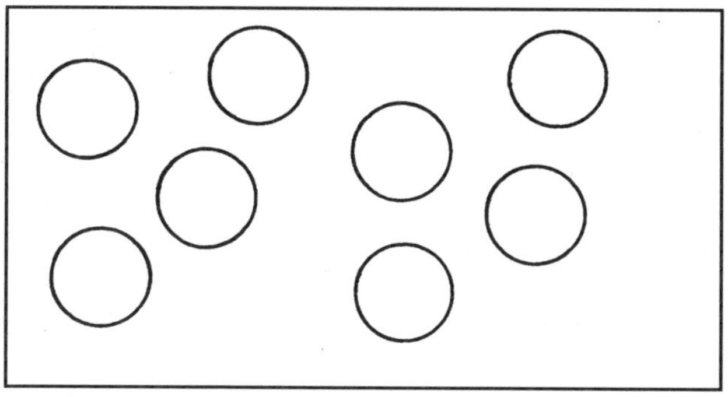

__________ of 8 is __________

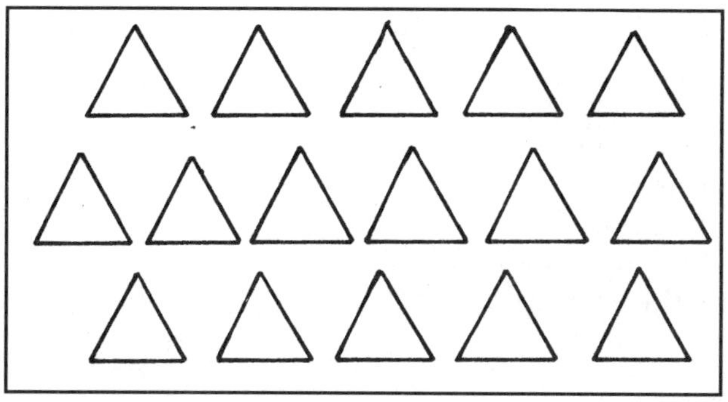

__________ of 16 is __________

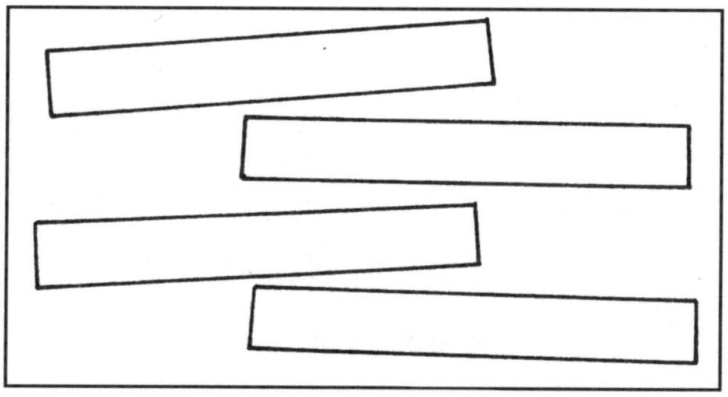

__________ of 4 is __________

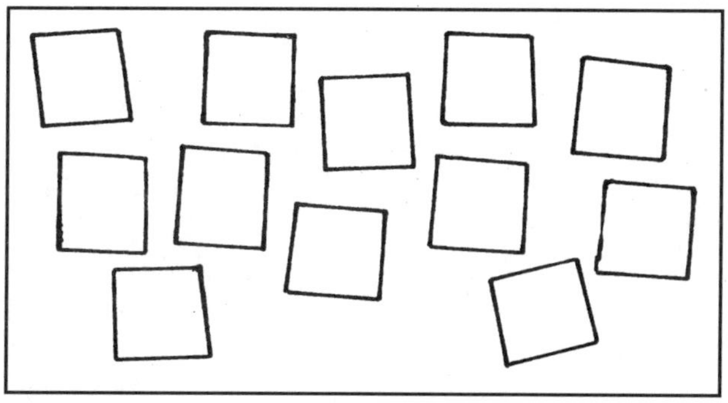

__________ of 12 is __________

REINFORCEMENT ACTIVITY

Uncover the board

Key aim

- To give practical experience of working with equivalent fractions ($\frac{2}{4} = \frac{1}{2}$).

What you need

- 1 copy of the activity sheet and 1 postermat (or the photocopiable version on page 48) for each child
- scissors
- scrap paper
- fractions dice (see below)

Organisation

- The children can cut out the game pieces before they start the activity, or after they have worked as a group to find equivalent fractions.
- Prepare a number of fractions dice by marking the six sides of blank dice or cubes: $\frac{1}{2}$ $\frac{1}{2}$ $\frac{1}{4}$ $\frac{1}{4}$ $\frac{1}{4}$ $\frac{1}{4}$.
- The children play the game in twos, threes or fours.

The activity

- Discuss with the children how they go about sharing things to eat – perhaps pizza, or a bar of chocolate. Are they aware of ways to divide things fairly?
- Use scrap paper to fold shapes in half and then into quarters, demonstrating that one half is equal to two quarters.
- Discuss with the children the equivalence between two quarters and one half, using language such as 'two quarters are the same size as one half of this shape'. It is important to do this with various shaped and sized pieces of paper to help the children realise that the concept of equivalence applies to fractions whatever the shape or size of the whole.
- Explain the game to the children, then demonstrate by playing it with one child before leaving them to play independently.
- When they have finished playing the game ask them to talk to you about what happened.

Extension ideas

- Let the children use pieces, boards and dice to develop their own fractions game.
- Find halves and quarters of sets of objects: 4... 8... 12... 16... 20 to develop the understanding that equivalence applies to sets and numbers as well as shapes and objects.

USING & APPLYING

COMMUNICATION

- Report orally on the results of playing the fractions game.

TALK ABOUT

- *'What fraction would you like to throw next time? Why?'*
- *'Is there another way to remove a half/two quarters?'*
- *'How much of your board is still covered?'*
- *'What fraction do you need to throw to finish?'*
- *'How could we make the game easier/harder?'*

HERE'S THE MATHS

- The idea of equivalent fractions takes a long time for children to understand, and they need to experience a range and variety of activities at each stage.

WHAT TO LOOK FOR

- Can the children say what fraction they need next to finish the game?
- Can they use the knowledge that two quarters are the same as one half?

MORE HELP NEEDED

- Do the activity with halves only.

Name ______________________

Uncover the board

Play this game with a partner.
Cut out the playing pieces from this page.
Fit them on top of the shapes on the postermat board.
Throw the fractions dice. If you get $\frac{1}{2}$, remove a piece which is half the area of the shape. If you get $\frac{1}{4}$, remove a piece worth a quarter of the area of the shape.
The first person to uncover the shapes on the board wins.

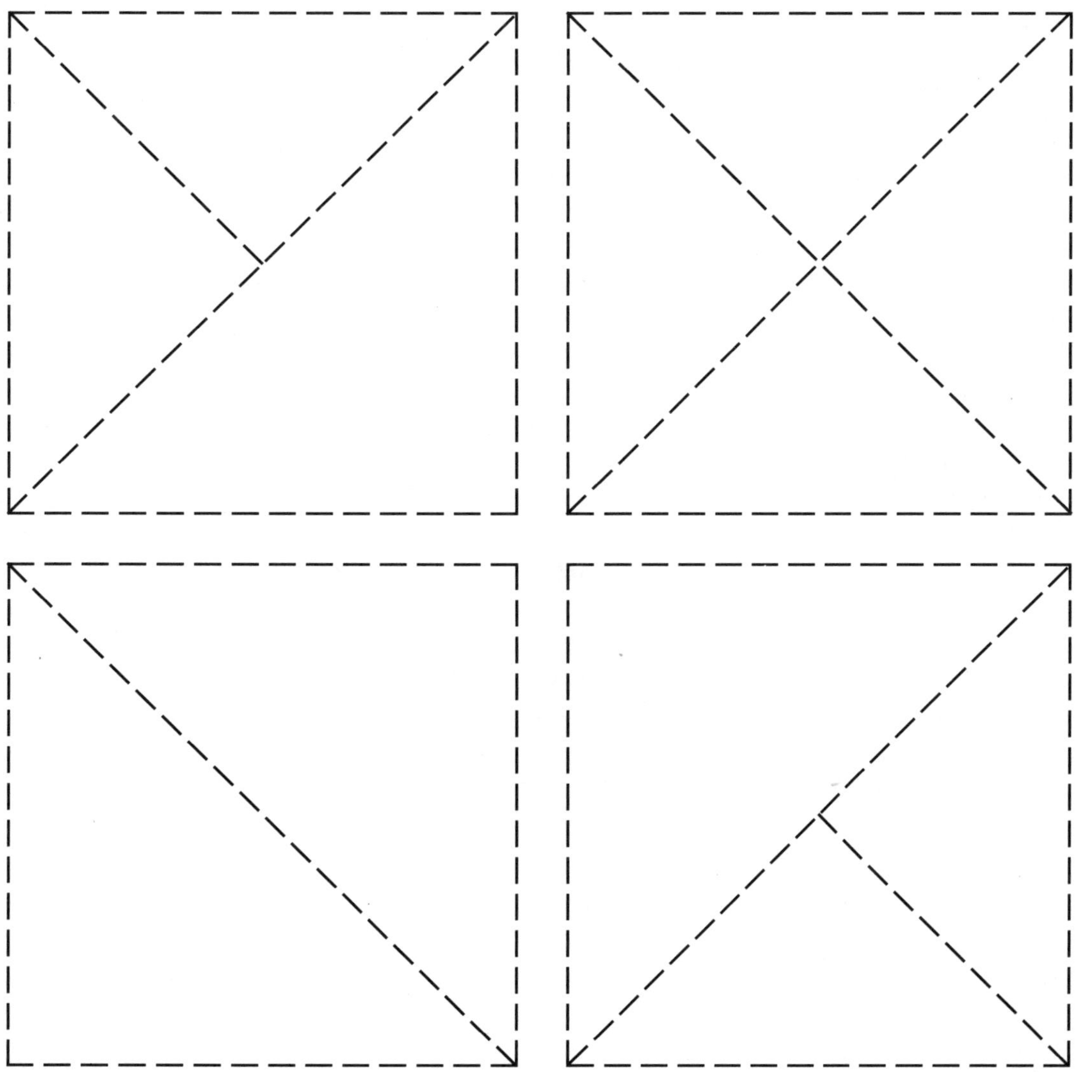

REINFORCEMENT ACTIVITY

How to find half

Key aims

- To give practical experience of halves, quarters and three-quarters of quantities (mass and length).
- To use a calculator for halving and quartering numbers.
- To explore the relative sizes of fractions.

What you need

- Plasticine or play dough and knives
- balances and/or scales
- calculators
- rulers
- 1 copy of the activity sheet for each child

Organisation

- Prepare space for the children to work with the Plasticine or play dough.
- Provide a variety of weighing apparatus so that the children can make their own decisions about which to use.

The activity

- Make Plasticine sausages of different shapes and sizes, then explore different ways to halve and quarter them. Encourage the children to use scales or balances.
- Introduce 'three-quarters' and encourage the children to notice that three-quarters is greater than a half.

Extension ideas

- The children could start by making a sausage with a mass of 200g, then repeatedly halve every subsequent sausage. Children could have a valuable discussion on the point at which this activity comes to a natural end. Each time the mass is halved use a calculator to divide by two to ensure that each 'half sausage' is equal.
- Try the activity again, but quarter the sausage this time. Use the activity sheet to record results.

USING & APPLYING

PROBLEM SOLVING

- Decide how to use calculators, rulers and weighing equipment to solve a problem.

TALK ABOUT

- *'What happens if you change the shape of one half of your sausage?'*
- *'Can you think of a fraction that is greater than a quarter... a half?'*
- *'If you cut off a quarter of this sausage what fraction is left?'*
- *'How can you check that you have divided the sausage fairly?*

HERE'S THE MATHS

- This activity is challenging because children must decide if half or quarter of the sausage is defined by size, by weight, or both.
- They also have to work out how to tackle the activity to get a reasonable result.

WHAT TO LOOK FOR

- Can the children find a way of dividing the sausage into equal fractions?
- Can they use mass to help solve the problems?
- Do they know what is meant by three-quarters?

MORE HELP NEEDED

- Children could start the activity by folding and shading paper strips to show halves and quarters.

Name ______________________________

How to find half

Make a sausage with a mass of 200g.
Halve it.
Use the calculator to help you decide how heavy it should be, then weigh it to check.
Halve it again.
Keep going for as long as you can.
Use the 'Halves' table to record your results.
Try again, but this time **quarter** the sausage.

Halves	

Quarters	

Would you rather have...?

Key aims

- To consolidate understanding of halves, quarters and three-quarters of objects, quantities and sets.
- To use a calculator to find half of a number.
- To develop the idea that the same fractions can be different sizes if the size of the whole is different.

What you need

- *Would You Rather?* by John Burningham (Picture Lions)
- a collection of 1p and 2p coins
- a range of small food items such as fruit, bars of chocolate, tubes of sweets, boxes of cereals
- calculators, balances and weights
- plain paper and pencils
- 1 copy of the photocopiable page for each child and blank sheets of paper

The activity

- Read *Would You Rather?* to the children, taking care to get them to make their own choices from the alternatives offered and explain their reasons. (If the book is not available the activity can be introduced by discussing choices.)
- Ask if they would rather have half of 12p or three-quarters of 8p. Use the coins to find which is more.
- Show the children one of the choices on the activity sheet and ask them to decide which they would choose. Discuss the choices made (they may choose a smaller fraction of one thing because they like it more than the alternative!).
- Encourage them to use the appropriate equipment to compare some fractions of the amounts, such as half of a 20 gram packet of sweets and a quarter of a 40 gram packet.
- Be sure to demonstrate how to use the calculator to find half of a number by dividing by two if the children do not come up with the idea themselves.
- When they have made a decision they should record it on a sheet of paper.

Extension ideas

- Discuss what would happen if the fractions were changed so that instead of having a quarter of the apples they had a half.
- Ask the children to make up their own choice questions as in *Would You Rather?* with the items available. They could create their own books and exchange them with a friend.

USING & APPLYING

PROBLEM SOLVING
- Decide how to use equipment to solve a problem.

COMMUNICATION
- Use the language of simple fractions.

LOGICAL REASONING
- Respond to 'What if...'. questions.

TALK ABOUT

- *'Why did you choose that one?'*
- *'How did you work it out?'*
- *'What could you use to help you find which is more/less?'*
- *'Why is half of this more than half of this?'*

HERE'S THE MATHS

- Children need to know that fractions only relate to the whole that they are part of, and that they do not have an absolute value, so:
  - half of 12p is different from half of 4p;
  - three-quarters of 4p is still less than half of 12p.

WHAT TO LOOK FOR

- Can the children see that a quarter of one quantity can be more than half of a different quantity?
- Can they find three-quarters of 8p?

MORE HELP NEEDED

- Simplify the problem by just comparing halves of different quantities at first, go on to quarters if the children cope well with that.

Name ______________________________

Would you rather have...?

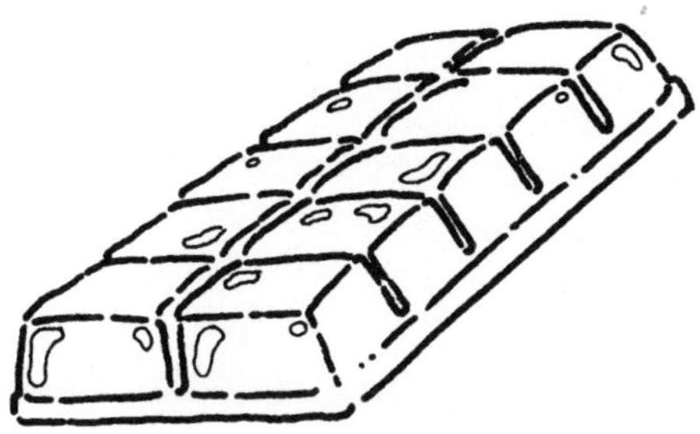

$\frac{1}{2}$ of this chocolate or $\frac{1}{2}$ of this chocolate

$\frac{1}{2}$ of this lemonade or $\frac{1}{4}$ of this milk

$\frac{1}{4}$ of these apples or $\frac{3}{4}$ of these bananas

$\frac{1}{4}$ of 20 pence or $\frac{1}{2}$ of 16 pence

USING & APPLYING

PROBLEM SOLVING
- Decide how to use coins in the context of a game.

LOGICAL REASONING
- Develop strategies for playing games.

TALK ABOUT

- *'Can you think of a way to make 10p with a smaller number of coins?'*
- *'Can you do it with 1 coin? 2 coins? 3 coins? 4 coins? 5 coins?...'*
- *'What do you need to throw next?'*

HERE'S THE MATHS

- It is important for the children to be able to use money in a flexible way, and to understand the equivalence and combinations of coins' values.

WHAT TO LOOK FOR

- Can the children find five different ways of making 10p?
- Can they calculate the amounts mentally?

MORE HELP NEEDED

- Ask the children to make 5p in as many ways as they can first.

Make 10p

Key aim

- To explore combinations of coins to 10p.

What you need

- selection of 1p, 2p, 5p, and 10p coins
- 1 copy of the activity sheet for each child
- bags or boxes to hold the coins
- a number of money dice showing 1p 1p 2p 2p 5p 10p

Organisation

- This game is best played by children in pairs or threes.
- Provide each group with a bag or box containing a range of the listed coins.

The activity

- Work with the group to find combinations of coins which make 10p.
- Hand out the activity sheets and read through the game instructions with the children.
- Demonstrate how to play the game 'Make 10p' on the activity sheet.

Extension idea

- Create two dice labelled 5p, 5p, 5p, 2p, 2p, 2p and 2p, 2p, 2p, 1p, 1p, 1p.
- Change the game board so that each card is labelled with 20p as the target value.
- Players take turns to roll both dice and then choose *one* of the following options:
  - collect both coins to match the two dice outcomes;
  - collect an appropriate coin from just one dice outcome;
  - pass if neither dice outcome is useful.
- The object of the game is, again, to fill all the game cards.

Name ________________________________

Make 10p

Take turns to throw the dice and collect the coin shown.

- You can put the coin on any card on your game board.
- If you cannot use it return it to the box or bag.
- The aim of the game is to be the first to make 10p in five different ways.

10p card

10p card

10p card

10p card

10p card

Shake the cup

Key aims

- To explore combinations of coins to 10p.
- To record coin values.
- To explore the equivalence of coins to 10p.

What you need

- a selection of 1p, 2p, 5p and 10p coins
- plastic cups
- 1 copy of the activity recording sheet for each child

Organisation

- Ensure that all the children can see and count the coins that are being used.
- Children should play the game in groups of three or four.

The activity

- Work with the group first, putting coins in the cup and shaking it.
- Ask the children how much they think is in the cup; they may tell you the number of coins or their value.
- Encourage them to combine these two aspects: 'you say that there are two small coins in the cup, what could they be... a 5p and a 1p... how much are they worth together? Could it be two 1ps?'

Extension ideas

- Ask each child to make 10p in a different way, each time counting the values into a plastic cup. Then check the amount by counting the coin values out of the cup.
- Lay the coins on a chart in four columns with the 10p, 5p, 2p and 1p headings.
- To make a permanent record, children could lay the coins under the sheet and make rubbings with gold and silver wax crayons.

USING & APPLYING

PROBLEM SOLVING

- Decide how to begin and organise a particular problem – finding the smallest number of coins for a given amount.

COMMUNICATION

- Record coin values.

TALK ABOUT

- *'How do you know which coins are in the cup if you can't see them?'*
- *'Does the size of a coin show how much it's worth?'* *'How many different ways can you make up 5p?'*
- *'How many different amounts can you make with just two of the coins?'*

HERE'S THE MATHS

- This activity helps children to become familiar with the value and appearance of coins, and encourages them to think about equivalent values.

WHAT TO LOOK FOR

- Can the children make an equivalent amount with different coins?
- Can they calculate flexibly and mentally?

MORE HELP NEEDED

- Use fewer coins.

Name ______________________________

Shake the cup

Put some coins in a cup, then shake it.
Ask the others in your group to guess how much money is in the cup.
Tip the cup and count the money – challenge the group to make the same amount with fewer coins.
Use the table to record.

Coins in the cup	Value	Coins we used to make the same amount

USING & APPLYING

PROBLEM SOLVING
- Decide how to begin a problem.

LOGICAL REASONING
- Make decisions about fractions.

TALK ABOUT

- *'What fraction will you hide next?'*
- *'How did you work out the hidden fraction that time?'*
- *'Can you hide a quarter of this set... a third... three-quarters?'*
- *'Why are 16, 20 and 24 good numbers of counters to choose?'*

HERE'S THE MATHS

- Finding three-quarters of a number of objects is challenging, and requires either a 'feel' for it (which is possible with small numbers), or systematic division into quarters, then combining three of those quarters.
- Discuss with the children the methods they are using.

WHAT TO LOOK FOR

- Can the children work out a quarter, half, and three-quarters of small numbers of objects?
- Can they guess how many are hidden when shown a quarter, half, and three-quarters of small numbers of objects?

MORE HELP NEEDED

- Restrict the problem to halves, initially.

Hidden fractions

Key aim

- To explore quarters, halves and three-quarters of sets and numbers.

What you need

- counters
- 1 copy of the activity sheet between each pair

Organisation

- The game is played in pairs.

The activity

- Show the children the activity sheet.
- Explain the game: 'If you choose a set of 12 counters, then hide six, your partner can look, and count, then decide "I think that six are hidden, and six is half of 12, so you hid half of the set."'
- Demonstrate how to play the game before leaving the children to play in pairs.

Extension ideas

- This activity reinforces the notion of fractions as part of a number, and introduces the idea of factors. Children could go on to choose a target number (such as 24) and explore it, using a calculator.
- Set the calculator to add 1 by entering 0 + 1 = = = = =
- Do you (eventually) reach 24?
- Start at 0 again, this time adding 2. Do you reach 24?
- Continue exploring with other numbers (each time starting from 0) to find out which numbers will 'hit' the target (in this case 24).

Name ________________________

Hidden fractions

Play this hiding game with a partner.

Choose a number of counters (6, 8, 16, 20, 24 are good numbers).

Take turns to hide a fraction of the set – then let the other person guess the hidden fraction.

Replace the counters once the fraction has been guessed.

When you have hidden as many fractions as you can from your set choose a different number of counters.

Fraction number lines

USING & APPLYING

COMMUNICATION
- Read, write and use the language of simple fractions in context.

TALK ABOUT

- *'Can you join the dots?'*
- *'What do you think the picture will be?'*
- *'Where would you put ½, or 1½, or 3½ on this number line?'*

HERE'S THE MATHS

- Placing fractions on a number line is an effective way of demonstrating that fractions are numbers which use the same operations of addition, subtraction, multiplication and division as the 'counting' numbers with which children are more familiar.

MORE HELP NEEDED

- Ask children to fold a strip of paper into halves and quarters and to mark the appropriate points on the strip.

Key aims

- To explore oral counting in fractional steps.
- To develop a mental model of number lines marked with fractions.
- To devise and construct number lines marked with fractions.

What you need

- 1 copy of the photocopiable sheet for each child
- scrap paper
- copies of the fraction number lines resource sheet (page 47)

Organisation

- Work through the first part of this activity with the whole group together. Children can then continue to work on the activity sheets individually.

The activity

- Play some games to develop the children's ability to count orally in fractional steps.
- This could be modelled with squared paper to show how it relates to the practical aspect of counting.
- Hand out the 'dot-to-dot' activity sheet and encourage the children to complete the picture, counting (quietly) in fractions as they do so.
- Children who complete the picture quickly can be challenged to complete the number lines on page 47.

Extension ideas

- Show the children what a half is on the calculator by dividing 1 by 2. Then clear the display and enter

0 + 0.5 = = = = = = =.

On most simple calculators this will have the effect of adding 0.5 each time. Once established this idea can be used to help the child create a decimal number line, perhaps using results in similar ways to the main activity.
- As a further extension, challenge the children to count on their calculators in quarters.

Name ______________________________

Fraction number lines dot-to-dot

Join the dots to complete the picture.

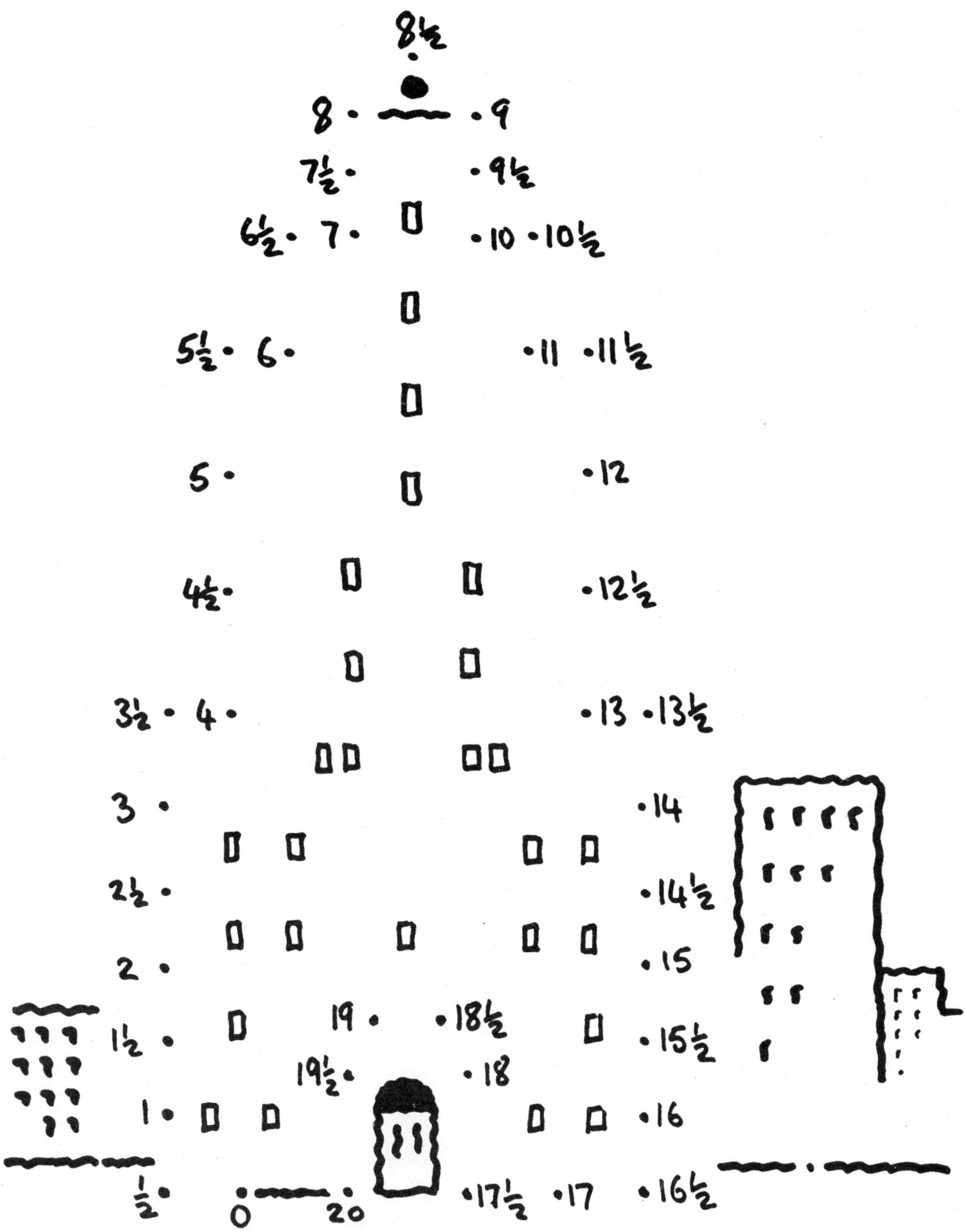

Coins in the circle

USING & APPLYING

PROBLEM SOLVING
- Finish a set task.

COMMUNICATION
- Discuss simple money problems.

TALK ABOUT

- *'Which coin are you going to put down next?'*
- *'If you put that coin in the circle how much will the pile be worth?'*
- *'How close are you to 20p now?'*
- *'Can you think of a way to win?'*

MORE HELP NEEDED

- Children who struggle with reaching 20p could try first to make 10p in coins.

Key aims

- To explore combinations of coins to specific values.
- To develop strategies for playing money games.

What you need

- selection of coins, predominantly 1p, 2p, 5p, 10p and 20p
- 1 copy of the activity sheet between two

Organisation

- Introduce the task to the whole group, then play the game in pairs.

The activity

- Provide a range of coins and explain the game to the children.
- Hand out the photocopiable sheets.
- Enter the value children should aim for – 20p would be appropriate as a starting point.
- The game is simple initially but once the children have played it a couple of times they will probably work out various strategies to ensure they put down the final coin. Encourage this.

Extension ideas

- Challenge children to make 50p (or other values).
- Select different coins for the children to work with.
- Ask them to write down their winning tips.

Name ______________________________

Coins in the circle

You can use 1p, 2p, 5p and 10p coins.
Try to make 20p exactly.
Take turns to put a coin in the circle
The person who puts in the last coin to make 20p exactly is the winner.

How much more?

Key aims

- To work with combinations of coins to £1.
- To give change for amounts to £1.

What you need

- scissors
- 1 copy of the activity sheet between each pair (enlarge this to A3 if possible)
- a sheet of blank paper for each child
- selection of coins
- number lines

Organisation

- The cards could be photocopied on to thin card instead of paper.
- Children should carry out the activity in pairs.
- Ensure that the children are aware of the values of the coins with which they will be working.

The activity

- Discuss the activity and show the children how, in shops, change is given by counting on from the cost of the item to the value of the coins given.
- A number line is useful for showing the jumps made.
- Explain how to play the game:
  - cut out the cards on the activity sheet and put them in a pile;
  - take turns to choose a card and work out how many more coins you need to make £1;
  - record the coins you used on your sheet of paper.
- Children should be allowed to find their own methods of recording; some may draw coins, others record values.

Extension idea

- The children could choose an amount, such as 61p, and find all the possible combinations for change to £1. Discuss which set of coins someone working in a shop is most/least likely to use and the reasons for this.

USING & APPLYING

PROBLEM SOLVING
- Decide how to use money to solve problems.

COMMUNICATION
- Invent simple ways of recording.

TALK ABOUT

- *'Could you think of another way of making that amount up to £1?'*
- *'Is that the smallest number of coins that you can use?'*
- *'Can you close your eyes and picture the coins that you need to find?'*

HERE'S THE MATHS

- Familiarity with coins and ways of making up amounts of money, is an essential part of shopping. Children should be aware that there are usually many different ways to make up each amount.

WHAT TO LOOK FOR

- Can the children make up £1 in several different ways?
- Are the children familiar with the value of all the coins?

MORE HELP NEEDED

- Work with smaller amounts of money.

Name ______________________

How much more?

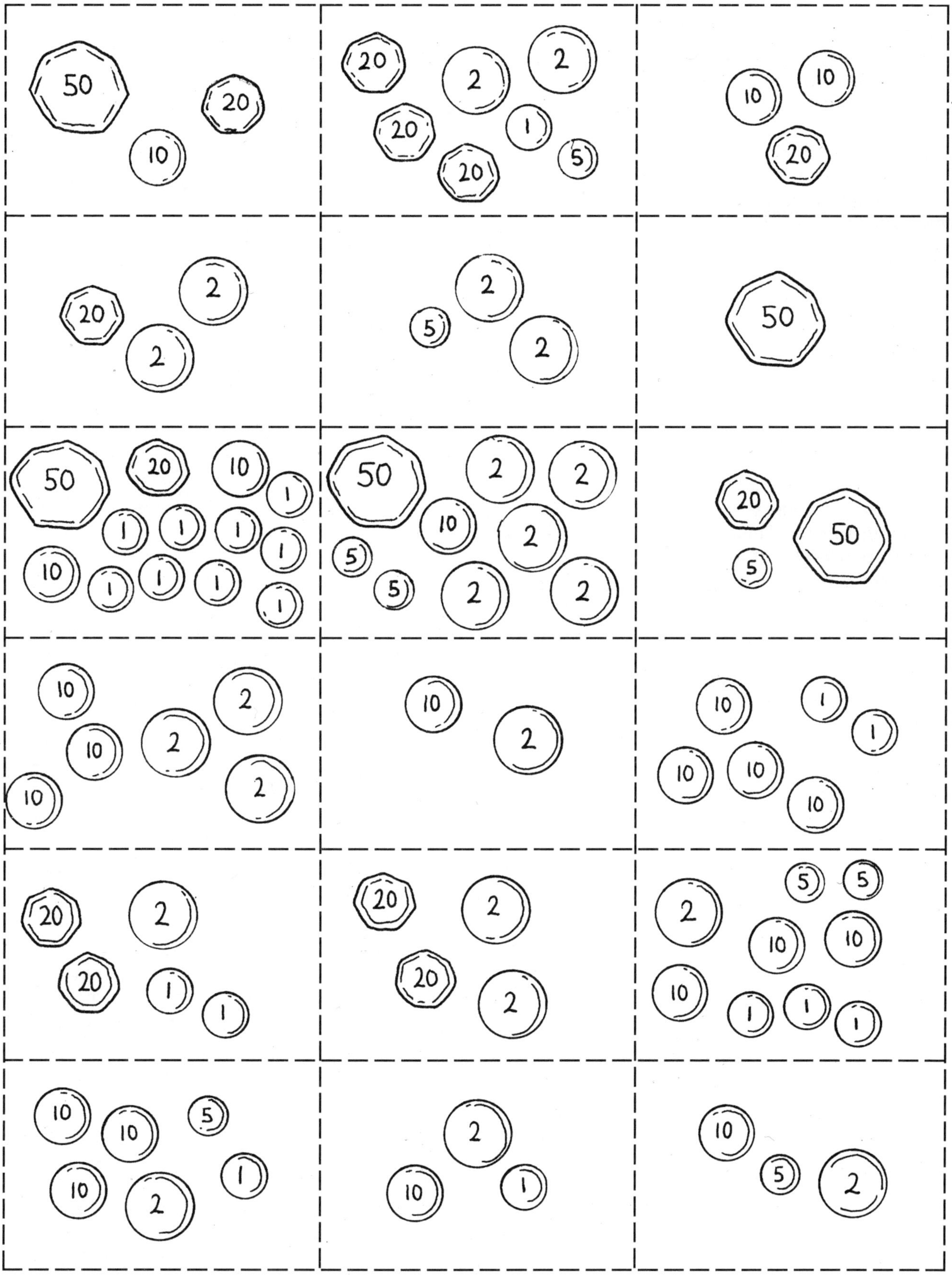

USING & APPLYING

PROBLEM SOLVING
- Follow rules and work independently within a group.

COMMUNICATION
- Respond appropriately to questions.

LOGICAL REASONING
- Predict who will win as the game proceeds.

TALK ABOUT

- *'Who is winning?'*
- *'How much more do you need to exchange for another 10p?'*
- *'How much do you need to win?'*

HERE'S THE MATHS

- Games provide a useful way of practising ideas with which children are becoming familiar. This game encourages children to count amounts of money quickly and accurately.

WHAT TO LOOK FOR

- Can the children work out the correct amount of money quickly?
- Do they appreciate the value of all the coins?

Build up game

Key aims

- To explore the idea of place value in the context of money.
- To introduce decimal notation through number.

What you need

- 1 (or more) water soluble or dry-wipe pen
- a £1 coin, a bag of 10p coins and a bag of 1p coins
- a dice labelled 2p, 2p, 5p, 5p, 1p, 1p

Organisation

- Prepare copies of the activity sheet game board by photocopying, then pasting them on to card. Cover these in clear adhesive film so that they can be reused on future occasions.
- Set up the coins in a central 'bank'.

The activity

- This game is designed for 2–4 players.
- Explain the rules to the children and help them through their first two goes. Once the game is underway many groups will be able to work independently, although some children may find the exchanging and recording problematic.
- Ask the children to write a zero in each box along the top row of their sheet to show they have no money.
- Tell them that they will take turns to roll the special dice and collect that amount from the central bank of money.
- When they have collected their money show them that they must place that amount in the right-hand box of their grid.
- They must then remember to write the total number of each type of coin they have in the top row of their game board using the dry-wipe pen.
- As soon as a player has gained ten 1p coins, these can be exchanged for a 10p.
- The 10p coins must be built up in the centre column to reinforce the importance of place value and the written recording along the top should always match the number of coins in each column.
- Play proceeds until one player has enough 10p pieces to exchange for the £1 coin.

Extension idea

- Children who work well and independently on this task could be encouraged to start at £1 and subtract amounts from their game board. This is more challenging but relies on the same process of exchange.

Name ______________________________

Build up game board

£	•	

Calculator decimals

USING & APPLYING

PROBLEM SOLVING
- Use the calculator correctly and follow appropriate lines of enquiry.

COMMUNICATION
- Discuss work with the teacher and other children.

LOGICAL REASONING
- Spot number patterns and make generalisations.
- Use mental methods to predict solutions.

TALK ABOUT

- *'What have you found out so far?'*
- *'Can you work this out without using your calculator?'*
- *'What method would you use to find half of 12, 13, 179, 4735?'*

HERE'S THE MATHS

- The connection between finding half of a number and dividing that number by 2 is sometimes a difficult one for children to understand. The calculator can provide a useful link, so that they establish for themselves that $\frac{1}{2}$ of 10 is 5 and that $10 \div 2 = 5$.

MORE HELP NEEDED

- Children who have difficulty understanding the notion of odd and even numbers should be encouraged to repeat the exercise, but this time with a sequence of consecutive numbers written down the first column for them.

Key aims

- To introduce decimal fractions.
- To observe patterns in number sequences involving decimals.

What you need

- 1 copy of the activity sheet for each child
- calculators, enough for one each, or one between two

Organisation

- Children could work in pairs to enhance the communication of ideas.
- They could be asked to give feedback to the rest of the group on what they have found out.

The activity

- Ask the children to write 10 in the first column of their activity sheet, then invite them to tell you what half of ten is.
- Show them how to check this by using the division key on the calculator.
- Do the same with 16 and observe them using their calculators.
- If they can press the appropriate keys, ask them to think of their own numbers (less than 100) and to record what half of their chosen number is.
- Once odd numbers are selected they will get answers ending in .5 and children may work out for themselves what this means.

Extension ideas

- Change the activity sheet so that the second column is headed 'Quarter the number', then repeat the activity. Children can later explore the effect of division by other numbers, such as 4 and 5.
- Children could be encouraged to divide numbers in sequence so that they can see the pattern in the answers:

$10 \div 4 =$
$9 \div 4 =$
$8 \div 4 =$

Name ______________________

Calculator decimals

Number	Half the number

USING & APPLYING

PROBLEM SOLVING
- Pick an appropriate piece and appreciate the strategies involved.

COMMUNICATION
- Ask and answer questions using the appropriate vocabulary.

LOGICAL REASONING
- Count on to calculate how much is required to finish.

TALK ABOUT

- *'What do the numbers 0.5 and 0.25 on this dice mean?'*
- *'How do you know that 0.25 is the same as ¼?'*

HERE'S THE MATHS

- It is important children understand that fractions and decimals are alternative ways of describing the same number. They need to appreciate the equivalence between ½ , 5/10 and 0.5. They will also learn that just as ½ + ½ = 1, so 0.5 + 0.5 = 1, and as ¼ + ¼ = ½, so 0.25 + 0.25 = 0.5.

WHAT TO LOOK FOR

- Do the children appreciate the connection between 0.5 and 0.25?
- Are they aware that 0.5 = ½ and 0.25 = ¼?

MORE HELP NEEDED

- Restrict the activity to halves, moving on to use quarters on another occasion.

Circle challenge

Key aims

- To develop an awareness and recognition of the decimal fractions 0.5 and 0.25.

What you need

- 1 copy of the activity sheet for each child
- a dice labelled 0, 0, 0.5, 0.5, 0.25, 0.25
- a supply of fraction pieces cut from the activity sheet pasted on card

Organisation

- This game is designed for 2–4 players. It should be fairly straightforward as it is essentially a matching activity.

The activity

- Explain the rules of the game to the children.
- The aim is to accumulate pieces and to build up whole circles from the fraction pieces. The winner is the first player to display six complete circles.
- Hand out the activity sheets and watch the children as they start to play.
- Encourage them to use the correct vocabulary as they take their pieces, and to say how many circles they have after each turn: 'I have taken a nought point five piece so now I have three point five circles.'
- The rules can also be varied.
  - They must build up one circle at a time and so may have to miss out on collecting if they throw a 0.5 but are waiting for a 0.25 to complete their circle.
  - Players may choose to throw the dice more than once when it is their turn, but they then lose all the pieces for that go if they throw a 0!

Name ______________________

Circle challenge

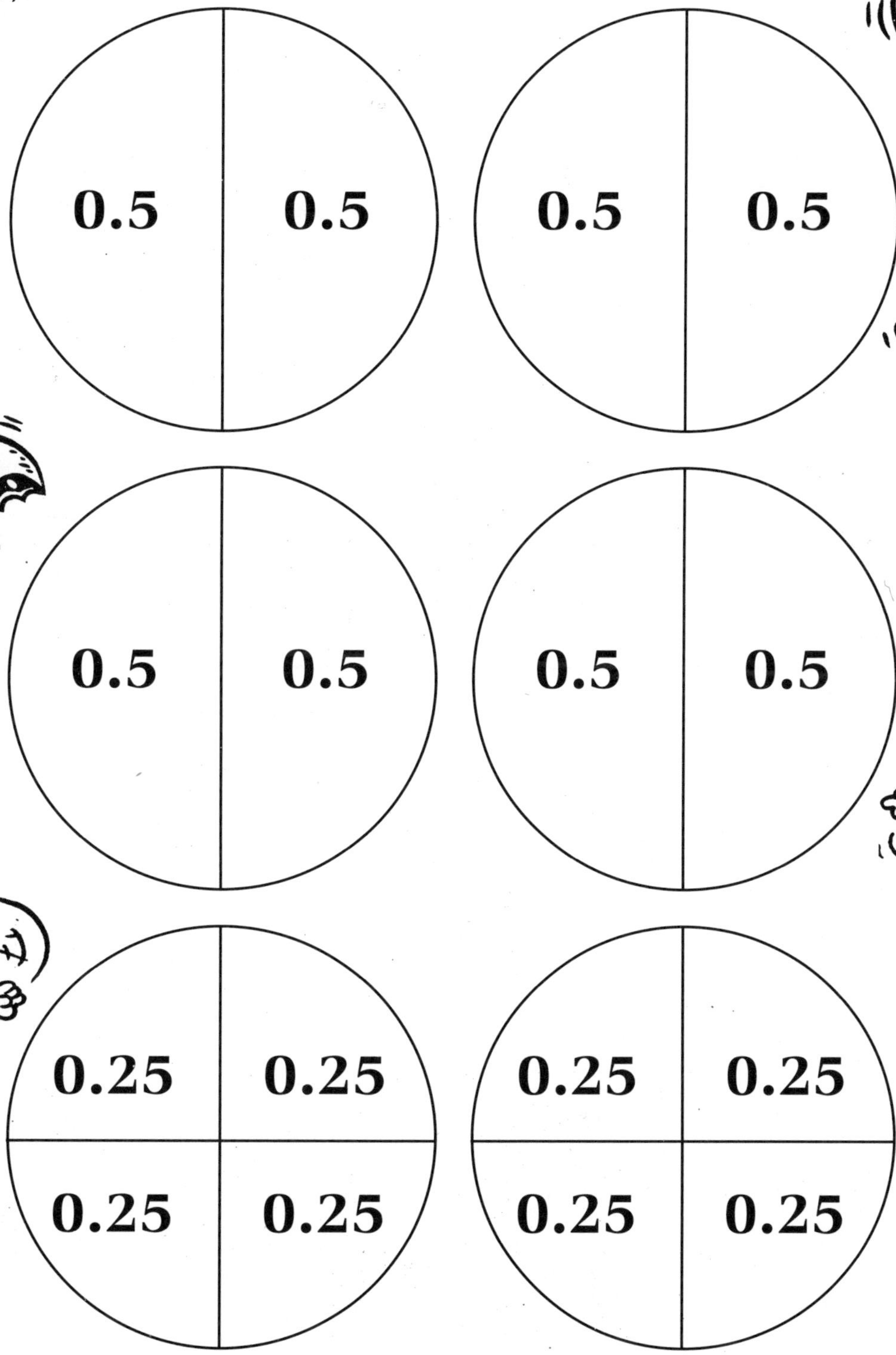

Take turns to roll the dice.

Take a piece to match your throw and fit it on to a circle.

The first person with six full circles is the winner.

Quarter cards

$\frac{1}{4}$	$\frac{1}{4}$	$\frac{1}{4}$	$\frac{1}{4}$
$\frac{1}{4}$	$\frac{1}{4}$	$\frac{1}{4}$	$\frac{1}{4}$
$\frac{1}{4}$	$\frac{1}{4}$	$\frac{1}{4}$	$\frac{1}{4}$
$\frac{1}{4}$	$\frac{1}{4}$	$\frac{1}{4}$	$\frac{1}{4}$
$\frac{1}{4}$	$\frac{1}{4}$	$\frac{1}{4}$	$\frac{1}{4}$
$\frac{1}{4}$	$\frac{1}{4}$	$\frac{1}{4}$	$\frac{1}{4}$

Fraction number lines

Write in the missing numbers on these lines.

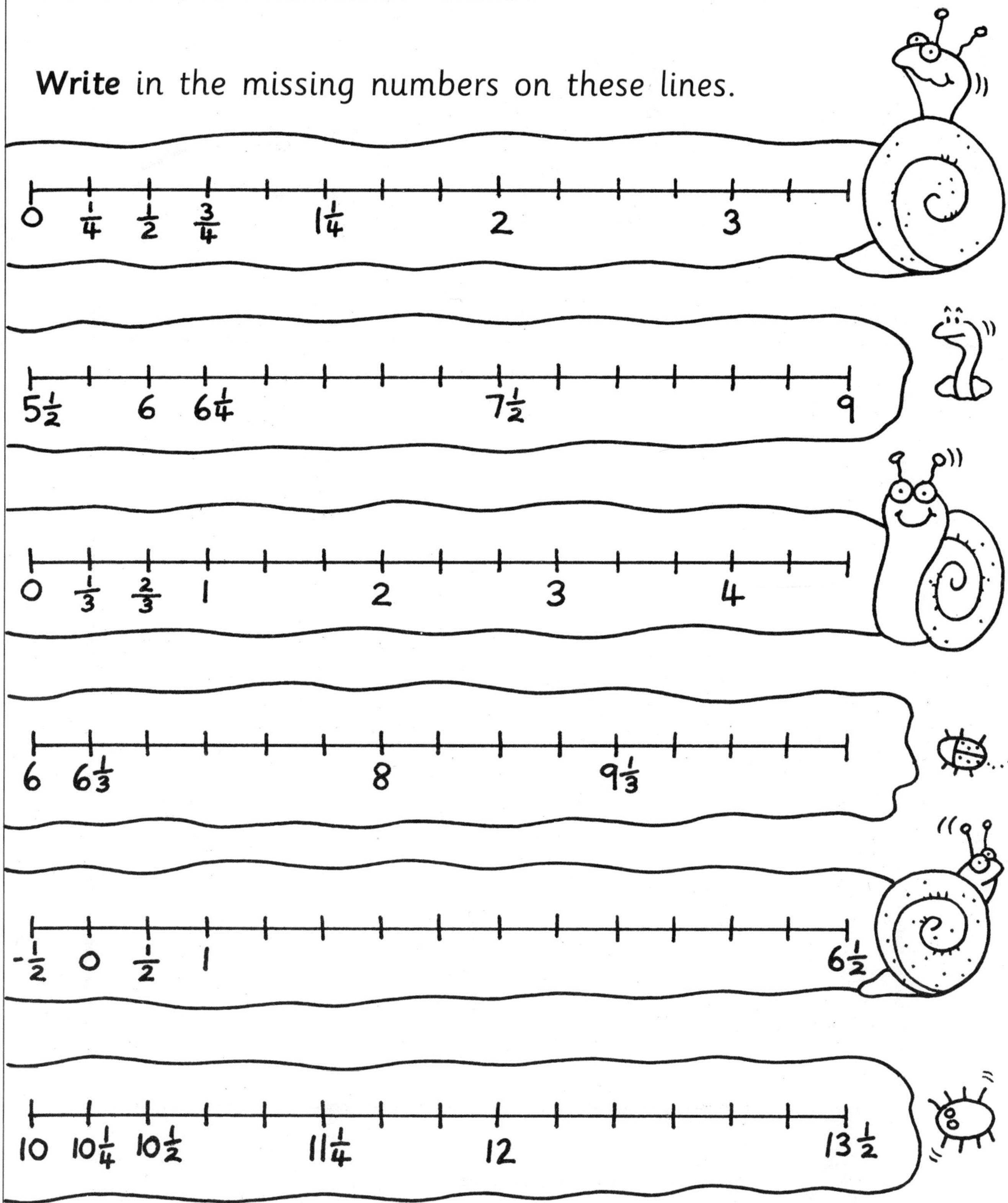

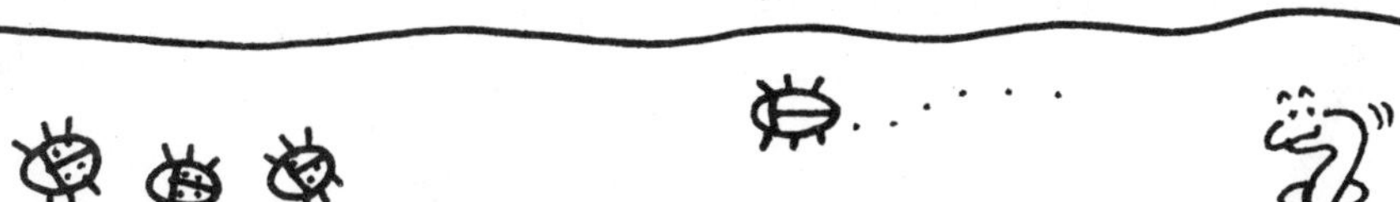

Make your own fraction number lines

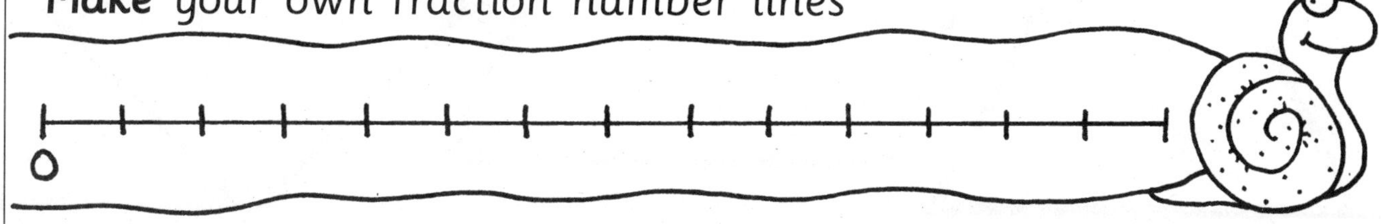